LISANNE

LISANNE
A YOUNG MODEL

by Betsy Cameron

Text by Diana Lewis Jewell

Foreword by Eileen Ford

DESIGNED BY BETTY BINNS

Clarkson N. Potter, Inc./Publishers NEW YORK

DISTRIBUTED BY CROWN PUBLISHERS, INC.

The photographs that appear in this book were taken by Betsy
Cameron with the exception of the following:
Pages 18, 168, 171, 172–73, and 174–75, Tom Sennett; Page 52, Al Rubin;
Page 116, Joe Gruszczynski; Page 158, Bob (Carmichle) Moore; Pages
154, 157, 160, 162 and 171, Uli Rose; Pages 166, 167, Les Goldberg.

Grateful acknowledgment is made to the following for permission to
reprint the photographs taken for advertisements: McCall Pattern
Company, page 117; Simplicity Pattern Company, Inc., page 117;
Danskin, page 117 (Bruce Weber photographer), page 117; Kodak (Ken
Ambrose photographer); to *Seventeen* Magazine for the photographs
on pages 117, 158, 159; and to Avon for the filmstrips on pages 138 and
139.

Published simultaneously in Canada by General Publishing
Company Limited.
First edition.
Printed in the United States of America

Library of Congress Cataloging in Publication Data
Cameron, Betsy.
    Lisanne: a young model.
    SUMMARY: Fourteen-year-old Lisanne Falk describes
her career as a photographic model.
    1. Falk, Lisanne.   2. Models, Fashion—United
States—Biography.   3. Youth—Employment—United
States.   1. Falk, Lisanne.   2. Models, Fashion]
I. Jewell, Diana Lewis.   II. Title.
HD6073.M772U54 1979   659.1'52   [B] [92]
ISBN 0-517-53866-0   79-17322

Contents

ACKNOWLEDGMENTS

When you put someone's life into pictures, you need cooperation of the closest, most personal kind. For this I thank Rose Falk and her daughter, Lisanne. Creating the pictures took energy, hours of work, a ton of understanding and a special kind of friendship.

Thanks also to Diana Jewell for her writing and her friendship through weekends, nights, all holidays, and lots of Famous Amoses!

For a first book to go from imagination to reality, it takes a lot of people with talent, patience, and wonderful faith. I thank in particular our agent, Connie Clausen, who was the first believer; the Clarkson Potter team of Jane West, Carol Southern, Nancy Novogrod, Pam Pollack, Michael Fragnito, and Nancy Kahan; Betty Binns, our designer, who put the pieces together so beautifully, and Betsy Nolan who sent us "on the road."

Ford Models, the agency both Lisanne and I call home, gave us both fantastic cooperation and moral support. Special thanks go to Jerry and Eileen Ford, Claudia Black, and all the bookers.

To enable me to shoot Lisanne on location, I was grateful for the help of Sam Alfstrad, Uli Rose, Robert Farber, George Rugen and Dolores Tucker of Alexander's, and Joe Gruszczynski and Lisa Rich of Macy's.

And, of course, there were the friends who listened, laughed, and helped—more than they know—Matt Jung, Tom Sennett, Leah Feldon, Bev Silver, and Kathy McCarthy.

And thanks to my family who encourage me in everything, so I'm never afraid to try.

Betsy Cameron

Foreword

Before you begin this exploration of what the life of a young model is like, I want to have a talk with you.

You're going to be reading about some very exciting experiences in the dual world of one special young lady, Lisanne Falk. And she handles both worlds exceedingly well. Because she keeps them separate. Her life as a "normal" fourteen-year-old at home and at school is every bit as important to her as her modeling career. And she tries not to let her assignments in front of the camera interfere with her studies, activities, or friendships. Lisanne is even a little bit secretive about her modeling successes!

And so it all works—for her. But that does not mean it is easy for every young person to maintain this harmonious balance between a normal home life and a hectic career world.

If you have an interest in pursuing this "double

life" as a model, your first consideration should not be, are you right for it. You must first ask yourself if it is right for *you*.

In order to help you with this important decision, I want to present a few of the very realistic considerations concerning the employment of children (even older children) as models. And I feel doubly qualified to do this. First, as Director-in-Chief of Ford Models, Inc. And, secondly, as the mother of four children, grandmother of two.

If I could offer advice to anybody interested in the world of young models, it would be first to parents. They must be aware of what this profession can do to a child—both physically and psychologically. First of all, whatever else modeling may be, it's work; and it can be more exhausting for a young person than an adult because children really have two careers. They go to school all day, and then they go to long (and sometimes difficult) bookings in their free time. Most children are pretty resilient, but parents have to keep a close watch and know their own child's limits.

Modeling can be hard on a young person emotionally as well. No matter how successful a model may be, there are still bookings she won't get, still jobs she'll not be right for. So there is a certain amount of rejection. It's normal. Parents must be aware of what repeated feelings of rejection will do to their child, especially in these formative years. Feelings of inadequacy or failure can last a very long time, and hurt is something we can all carry with us throughout a lifetime.

Some of the young models I've known feel they've failed their mothers when they lose a booking, because some may be modeling to make their mothers proud. In order for parents to fully under-

8

stand what rejection means to their child, it's extremely important that they know what motivates their child to want to model in the first place.

Of course, modeling places extraordinary emphasis on physical attributes. Not on beauty, necessarily, but certainly on height, weight, the set of one's eyes, the width of one's nose, the straightness of one's teeth. Preoccupation with any of this is dangerous—for both young and adult models! There is a greater concern with young children because they are impressionable, and because they have not fully formed their own code of values. A child might begin to believe that approbation is directly related to physical attractiveness. Again, this is something parents must guard against, both in their attitudes and the child's. Any implication that beauty and success are synonymous fosters unrealistic expectations that can thwart a child later in life.

The financial rewards of modeling certainly can be beneficial to a youngster, but it is the parent who must exercise great responsibility here. Putting a healthy percentage of the money away for an education is probably the most sensible thing parents can do. Once a child's modeling career is over, opportunities for personal growth should not be. Indulging the child is probably the worst thing to do with the money. Having too much too early is never helpful. It's even worse if there are brothers or sisters. If the young model's career (or earnings) makes her the "special" one in the family, all the children will suffer.

I would say if there's a good, close parent-child relationship; if the child is pretty levelheaded; and if she's doing well enough in school so that energies directed elsewhere will not make it hard for her to keep up with her class, then there is a chance for that child to be happy in the modeling world.

Still with me? If these first, and extremely important, considerations present no second thoughts for you, then it's time to take a look at your qualifications. Of course, there are some very specific physical requirements. You can't get around those. And with children, the requirements are much more stringent than they are for adult models. The women in our adult division, for instance, have to be fairly standard in dress size, and at least 5′ 7″. But a child model must be a certain size at a certain age. A ten-year-old, for example, should be a child's size 10. After size 10, the model is considered in a preteen category, provided she's reached at least 5′ 4″. Of course, there are always exceptions. Preteen is a very difficult group to cast. We only take about five or six girls in that range. If a girl's 5′ 5″, it's her last year in the Children's Division. If she's 5′ 7″, she's an adult model. I guess that means 5′ 6″—and you're out! (Don't despair. Some girls will work at 5′ 6″, but only if they have absolutely fantastic faces, and they don't count on many fashion bookings!)

It's not a grim life for a child to be a model. Just ask them! Most of Ford's children think it's glamorous—or at the very least, fun. And it can be, but the child learns quickly enough that it's not play. A model, no matter how young, is expected to be businesslike and thoroughly professional. Nobody books a girl because she's the cutest little thing they've ever seen!

Once a girl becomes a successful child model, there is still no guarantee that she'll make the transition into a successful adult model. In fact, very few do. For one thing, the child simply may not grow tall enough. Even if she does, she may have developed modeling habits through so many catalogue bookings that she may only be able to do catalogue work as an adult. This is not just typecasting. It's a completely different style of modeling—and it's difficult to switch into a less stylized technique.

We become very involved with a girl who is going through this period of transition. Usually, there's a break between her last assignments as a child model and her first attempts in the adult category. During that time, we'll send her out for new test shots. Then we'll analyze those to see what's working and what's not. We base our comments on the pictures exclusively, not on the girl. We judge only what the camera sees because it's the camera that determines everything for a model. How you photograph is what you are. A girl might think she's thin, but if the camera shows she's not, she's not.

It's the camera that sees—immediately—the special, intangible qualities, too. And you can spot these a mile away. They're what make some pictures jump off the page, and some just sit there. There are people and there are stars, and it's the camera that picks up the difference right away.

Lisanne Falk has this star quality. There's something absolutely magnetic about her eyes. She's got a pizazz, an upbeat, sparkling quality that comes through to the camera. That's what makes all the difference. Some models project so well because of an inner sense, a certain communion with the camera. Maybe that's what makes Lisanne the top child model at Ford right now. Will she make the transition? Well, first she has to grow two and a half inches. Then, we'll see. . . .

LISANNE

The real me

This is me. My name's Lisanne Falk. I guess the first things I should tell you are that I'm fourteen, in the ninth grade, love sports, playing the piano, and going to concerts. My favorite group is the Rolling Stones. I also like going to the movies, beach parties, and any shade of blue. I can live without school at times—but who can't. My friends and I aren't into heavy dating (yet)! We mostly go out in groups. Sure, someday I plan to get married and settle down with a couple of kids, but I don't have to think about that for a while. A long while. Probably none of that makes me very different from any fourteen-year-old. But, after school, I lead another life. I'm a model. Most of my friends think modeling must be fun. Most of my mother's friends think I work for a living. And I guess they're both right. It is a lot of fun. And it is a lot of work.

I'm wearing a Ford T-shirt because that's the name of the modeling agency I'm signed with. It's a pretty famous one, so I feel lucky that I've been with them since I was ten years old. And in four

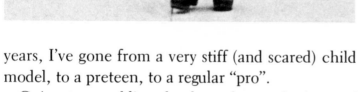

years, I've gone from a very stiff (and scared) child model, to a preteen, to a regular "pro".

Going to a public school on the south shore of Long Island and working as a photographic model in New York makes me feel like I live in two completely different worlds. And, so far, I think I've got

16

the best of both. It's fun to be in school one minute
and on the set the next. I can have twice as many
experiences and twice as many friends.

Now that I'm changing and growing up, my career is changing, too. A lot of what's been happen-
ing lately has to do with my friend, Betsy Cameron.

She's also a model. (I tease her and call her an older model.) But she is kind of like a big sister. Betsy's been modeling since she was seventeen. She's been on lots of covers, and she travels, and goes on location trips, and does commercials—lots of things I like to do. So she sort of shows me the ropes and gives me advice—on everything. Even what to do if I get a pimple. (She's got this magic overnight drying lotion from Europe that really makes it vanish overnight.)

When I can stay in New York, Betsy lets me stay at her place. So what do we do? Spend most of our time taking pictures. Not that I can't get enough of being in front of a camera. It's just that Betsy's been working on a second career as a photographer. In fact, the picture on the cover is the first shot she ever took of me, when I was twelve. Our friendship has really developed because we're both at the point where we're discovering new things about ourselves and what we can do. Sometimes, it's like there's not even a difference in our ages (until she has to call my mom to get permission for me to go somewhere!)

I never know what's going to happen next. Except I'll grow up. I hope that means growing two and a half more inches. I'm 5′ 4½″ now, and I know I should be at least 5′ 7″ to go on modeling in the Women's Division. Or maybe I'll go to college and study archaeology. (One good thing about modeling is that you can put the money away for school.) I'm not sure yet if I want to make this a permanent career. But it's a lot of fun right now. If you've ever wondered what it's like, or what you have to know, or what you have to do, this book is just for you.

Inside the
Ford Agency

If you want to work as a model in a city like New York, you really have to be signed with an agency. Sure, some magazines will use "real girls" (that's what they call nonprofessional models), but usually only once. Then they want you to be with an agency. Even if a brand new model walked in off the street, they'd probably send her to an agency before they'd book her.

That's good, because an agency really protects a model. There are certain rules which spell out specifically how and when a model can be booked and how much she should be paid. If a hairdresser has to work on you before you can get to work, you get paid for the time it takes. If you have to spend a day traveling to a location shooting, you get paid for your time. If a client keeps you overtime, after 5:30 P.M., you get paid time and a half. If a model chooses to do lingerie shots, she gets a higher fee than usual. So a client must state in advance if the model will be asked to wear lingerie at the shooting. That way, nobody gets surprised.

Except I did once. I agreed to do a bra ad for a client I had worked with for a long time. I knew them pretty well, and they promised me the ad

would be in a place nobody I knew would see. Well, of course, one of the boys at school saw it and brought it into class and showed it around. I won't do lingerie again—at least not while I'm still in school!

Agencies help models, and work to get them work. For this service, they charge both the model and the client a fee. Of course, commissions and regulations can vary from agency to agency, so you should investigate all the details before you sign with anyone. You also have to make sure it's an established, reputable agency. The big ones in New York and other large cities are all well known by photographers, advertisers, and editors. They're the agencies these people call regularly for models, so they can get you the most work.

Ford is the largest modeling agency in the world. But it's not impersonal, or snobbish, or anything. Eileen and Jerry Ford, the owners, are like the super-parents of one gigantic family. They even throw Christmas parties for all the kids in the Children's Division. Everybody's friendly—and there's always somebody to talk to if you need advice.

It makes me feel good to say "I'm with Ford." Everybody in the business knows that's the top. And Betsy's with Ford, too. So it makes it fun.

A lot of people think that since Ford is such a well-known agency, it only handles famous models. But that's not true. They're always looking for new discoveries. If they like your look—even if you've never modeled before—they'll take you on. It's a little different for older models. If they don't like a girl's look, but think she has potential, they'll send her to hairstylists, different photographers, and work with her until they like what the camera sees. Then they'll sign her. Sometimes, they just tell a girl to lose twenty pounds and come back. Can you believe it—that's what they first told Betsy! She was working as a showroom model, for Catalina bathing suits, when a model from one of the shows brought her to the agency. Eileen took one look at Betsy in her tent-shaped mini dress and long platinum blonde hair, and told her she'd have to lose weight if she wanted to be a photographic model. Betsy remembers sitting there wishing she had a portfolio full of beautiful pictures, like all the other girls. (Portfolios are like big scrapbooks filled with pictures. Models call them their "books," and carry them everywhere.)

But you don't need professional pictures, or portfolios, or experience when you first come to Ford. To get in the Children's Division, you can just send in some recent photos. My career really began as an accident. A friend of my mother's told her friend Kathy Dowd, a TV children's manager, about me when I was seven years old. She signed me and I'm still with her for TV commercials and movies. I lucked out on my first TV interview and got it. Then Kathy kept sending me on many more interviews, but I was so shy we decided to stop.

Kathy called us up a few years later to ask if I wanted to try again. My mom and I figured why not! At one of the interviews, a casting director said she thought I should try fashion modeling, and recommended Ford's Children's Division. (It was only one year old at the time.) Mom didn't take it seriously, but I kept asking her to send my picture in. Six months later, when we had a good photo (and it was a 99¢ supermarket special), she finally sent it. This is it, taken when I thought all you had to do in front of a camera was smile. Claudia Black, head of the Children's Division, liked it. After mom and I went in for an interview, she signed me right away, and two weeks later, I was working.

There's a lot more to an agency than just models. It's a business. And there are several different divisions behind the scenes at Ford.

For instance, there's the "Low Board." Models in the Women's Division who are just starting out and have to get a lot of pictures of themselves for their portfolios start in this division. The bookers on the board take the calls, make the appointments, and generally help the new girls get together with photographers for test pictures.

When you start really working, your chart moves to the "High Board." A chart is your own weekly calendar that the bookers fill in with your assignments, go-sees, fittings, or whatever you're doing. A model can choose not to accept assignments for a certain day, week, month, or longer. That's what's called booking out. For some bookings, the agency will have to ask the model first if she wants to do it. For me, they always put "ask first" beside any that would conflict with school. Clients can book you tentatively, and they can cancel no later than twenty-four hours before. Once they've changed a tentative booking to a definite one, they have to pay you even if they cancel. For every booking, the agency will write the photographer's name, address, client, and what, if any, wardrobe is needed. That's the info they'll tell my mom when she calls in. You never know for sure what's up until you call in at 5:00 P.M. the night before for your next day's assignments.

In addition to the bookers for photographic modeling, there's a TV department at Ford's. They handle the models for commercials. You have to belong to a union called SAG (Screen Actors Guild) to do TV work. You don't if you model for "print." That's what they call magazines, newspapers, and catalogues. A client can hire you one

26

time for a commercial if you're not in the union. But, after that, you pay your dues and join so you can do more and more and more.

The accounting department keeps track of billing the clients and paying the models. After every booking, we fill out a voucher (that's a bill for your time), then they take care of collecting the money. Sometimes it takes months for a client to pay. But what's really good is Ford pays us right away, weekly. Another good thing about the accounting department is that they keep 20 percent of your pay in reserve. That comes in handy when it's time to pay taxes. It's also kind of a financial safeguard for the future. Some models make a lot of money, but they don't make plans for what to do when their modeling careers are over. And even the most successful careers only last a certain time. It's a hard business to grow old in! Like athletes, models are paid very well, but they have only a few years to make their money. Betsy's taught me that it's best to have some idea of what you want to do next in life. Eventually, all models have to do something else. So I'm saving what I make for college.

The Men's Division handles—naturally—the male

models. Some of them are really cute. A lot of the models in the agency are friends outside of work, and some of them even date. That's why it's fun to stay at Betsy's. I get to meet models in real life! We go to this restaurant called Jimmy's, where everybody hangs out. Or we go to Ford baseball games. The Men's Division has their own team and they play other agencies and company teams in Central Park. They usually win, too! One of their biggest rivals is another modeling agency. Everybody turns out for those games.

This is my division right now. Yup—I'm still in the Children's Division. And I guess I will be until I grow some more. Claudia says height is a big determining factor between being in the Children's Division or going into Ford Women. I've grown taller than Claudia now, but I'm still not tall enough. Oh well, at least she tells me that I'm the Top Kid.

Claudia's really helped me develop as a model since she first signed me. And she's watched me go through a lot of changes—good and bad. When I

The Blob

The Blob finally relaxes

first started modeling, I was so inexperienced, I just
didn't know how to move. One of the earliest clients to book me, Alexander's, nicknamed me The
Blob because I just stood there. But I guess they
liked me anyhow, because they kept booking me.
As you can see, over the years, they really taught
me a lot. These are some of the Polaroids from my
earliest Alexander's shootings right up through recent ones.

I have fun at the shootings now because, after
four years, I pretty much know what I'm doing and
can relax.

It's great to have clients who use you over and
over again. But in order for these clients to book
you, they have to see you. So agencies are constantly sending out head sheets or composites of
their models to photographers, editors, advertising

The Blob moves

The Blob grows up

agencies, or anybody else who might be a prospective client.

A head sheet just shows a very small head shot of everybody in each division. This is usually the first thing a client will look through when he's searching for a new face. Say he finds you. But he still may not book you without seeing more than just that one shot. So the agency sends out your composite.

A composite is a small folder printed with four or more pictures. Usually a full-length shot, a good clear closeup, and others that show as many different looks as possible. It also includes "vital statistics" like weight, sizes, hair and eye color—and height.

Having just the right composite is really important to a model's career. A client looks at it and

THE FOLLOWING MODELS WILL BE AVAILABLE THROUGH 688-8544

MAUDE ADAMS

5'9" 8-10 9½
Excellent Legs
Dark Blonde/Blue *

INGRID ANDERSON

5'8" 6-7-8 9B $100/600
Dark Blonde/Green

MELODY ANDERSON

5'8" 9-10 8½ $100/600
Blonde/Green *

PAM ANDERSON

5'7½" 7-8 7½-8 $100/600
Blonde/Hazel *

ASHLEY

5'9" 10 8n $100/1000
Excellent Hands & Legs
Dark Brown/Blue *

SUZANNE BARNES

5'7½" 8-9-10 8b $100/600
Blonde/Blue

JAYNE BENTZEN

5'8" 8-9-10 7½ $100/600
Dark Blonde/Green *

JENNIFER BERRINGTON

5'9" 8-9-10 7 $100/750
Light Brown/Hazel *

DEBARA BERTIN

5'9" 8-9 8b
Blonde/Green

BITTEN

5'9" 8-10 7½ $150/1000
Blonde/Blue

ANNA BJORN

5'7" 6-7-8 7 $100/750
Blonde/Blue-Green *

KAREN BJORNSON

5'9½" 8 8
Blonde/Dark Blue

COLETTE BLONIGAN

5'9" 10 8½m $100/600
Blonde/Blue *

LESLIE BRANNER

5'9" 8-10 8 $100/750
Dark Brown/Brown

DENISE BROWN

5'8" 8 7½ $100/600
Brown/Brown

KAREN BRUUN

5'7" 5-7-8 7½b $100/750
Blonde/Green

CHERYL BUELL

5'7" 5-7-8 8 $100/600
Brown/Blue *

PIA BUGGERT

5'7½" 7-8-9 7½ $100/750
Blonde/Green *

BETSY CAMERON

5'7" 7-8-9 7b $100/750
Excellent Legs
Blonde/Blue

KAREN CAPONETTO

5'8" 7-8 8m $100/750
Dark Blonde/Blue

VALERIE STEIKER
Hair: Black Size 8

KIM CERTOS
Hair: Blonde Size 10

LOLLY BLODGETT
Hair: Blonde Size 10-12

LISA CICCONE
Hair: Strw. Blonde Size 10

SUZANNE FIERO
Hair: Red Size 10

JACQUI FITZPATRICK
Hair: Brown Size 10

TINA FOX
Hair: Blonde Size 10

TARA KRAWCHUK
Hair: Blonde Size 10

LISA MARTINIDES
Hair: Dk. Blonde Size 10-12

SUELAIN MOY
Hair: Black Size 10-12

ELIZABETH REIBSTEIN
Hair: Brown Size 10

SUZANNE MAREK
Hair: Brown Size 12

LEAH BATTELLE
Hair: Brown Size 12-14

JOANNE BLODGETT
Hair: Blonde Size 12-14

KENDRA BROWN
Hair: Brown Size 12-14

LISANNE FALK
Hair: Lt. Brown Size 14
preteen 8-10

makes a decision to have you come for a go-see or book you, or forget you. It's a good idea to get the best advice you can when you're selecting your pictures for the composite. Everybody was in on choosing mine—me, Claudia, and Betsy. They all know better than I do what people look for.

This is my first official adult-looking composite. Before, I just had 8 × 10 glossies to show. A child model can just show different shots of herself being a kid; here I am jumping, here I am standing still, here I am in a dress—that sort of thing. But as you get older, the competition gets tougher, and you've got to show that you can do more.

There are some models who are famous for just one look. But they don't get bookings unless the client wants that one look. So, in a composite, it's smart to show a variety of expressions. Since you never know what each client may be looking for, the best thing a model can be is versatile. Of course, your own special image must come through. Clients tend to typecast, and if they can't figure out what category a girl fits into, they're likely not to remember her when it comes time to book someone.

You might never know if a client liked your composite, and filed it away for future reference. Just because you're not used for one job doesn't mean you won't be considered for another one. Of course, you could be booked right after the client sees your composite. Or you could be asked to send your portfolio over to the client so they can see even more shots of you. If the client still isn't sure about you after all this, he might ask to see you—in person. No matter how you're selected, if you're right for the clothes—or the product—you'll get booked. And that's when your job really begins.

36

THE FORDS

388-7613

S.A.G.

HAIR: Dk. Blonde

EYES: Brown

SIZE: Jr. 5-7

SHOE: 6½-7

MY FIRST REAL COMPOSITE

Shooting a fashion ad

A model can be booked for just a few hours, a half day, a day, or more. The agency will let you know how long you'll be working for a client and what time the booking begins. It's up to you to show up on time and ready to work. There is a saying, "Time is money." Well, that's really true in this business. Models get paid by the hour. Stylists get paid by the hour. Photographers get paid by the hour. And the client may get very nervous if it looks like anybody's wasting time. If a model gets a reputation for being slow, or being late, or taking too much time to get ready, she stops getting bookings. And there's always someone out there to take her place.

So the first thing I do when I get to the studio is let them know I'm there, then head straight for the dressing room.

Usually, the stylist is already there, getting all the clothes ready. She has to unpack them, line them up in the order they're going to be photographed, get all the accessories together for each outfit, and even iron the clothes if they have any wrinkles that will show up in the pictures.

She'll show you what you're going to be wearing, so you can start getting into the mood—and into your makeup. Sometimes there are makeup artists

40

to help. But when there aren't, you have to do your own. I'm always picking up makeup tips from everyone—other models, magazines, editors. There's a style in makeup, just like in fashion, and it's up to a model to know what's new first, before the general public sees it. This is just part of being professional. You should know what you're doing.

You have to know how to fix your hair, too. I always check out what I'll be wearing to see if I need to get my hair off my shoulders to show off a special collar or neckline. Sometimes the stylist will tell you how she wants your hair.

On this shooting, the stylist is Bevie. She's up on all the latest fashion trends and knows how all the newest accessories should be worn. She even gave me her own bow tie for these shots because it looked right for this outfit. Basically, a stylist has to see that the clothes look really good for the camera. And they sure don't always fit the way they end up looking! If the pants are too long, she'll roll them up and pin them. Or maybe turn them under, and put in an instant hem with double-edged tape. If they're too baggy, she'll pin them in with what they call T-pins (big pins that look like the letter T and hold more than straight pins). Or the stylist can bunch the clothes up in the back and clamp them with clothespins or actual metal clamps. With all the pinning and pulling and clamping, you may get jabbed every once in a while, but the stylist usually feels worse about this than you do! Some models really can't stand people fussing with them like this all the time, but it's something you have to get used to. There are times you get stuffed with plastic or lined with tissue to make things look right. Or you might even get a necklace taped to your neck. As long as the camera can't see any of

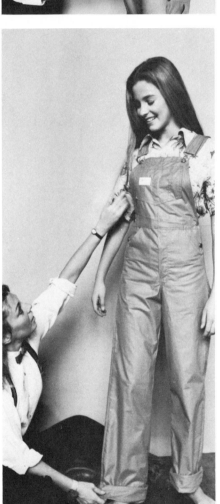

the "alterations," the shots will be okay. These are all things a model has to think about when she's on the set. You've got to move, but you can't let any of that show.

When I'm all ready, I go out to the set. The stylist will follow me out, with *more* pins (in case anything comes loose), and hairbrushes, and maybe a few more accessories to change as we shoot. I'll let the photographer know when I'm ready, but he may not be ready for me. There are still lots of things to check before we begin. So I just wait patiently and try not to mess up any of my pinnings, accessories, hair, or makeup. You have to stay just the way they fixed you. One thing you can't do is sit down—it causes wrinkles.

Everybody in the business knows the story about a stylist who tried to fix last-minute wrinkles on a model by trying to steam the clothes right on her. The model got burned—and the studio got sued. So if you get wrinkled, you have to take everything off for ironing, then start all over again.

The photographer and assistants will be setting up lights and strobes. They look like giant umbrellas. They're used to soften and bounce the light, so I'll look good.

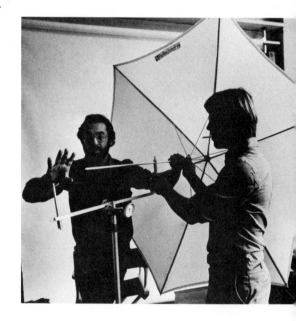

If there's no special background or props, I'll stand on no-seam paper. That's just a big, wide roll of paper that pulls down to give a plain background. You have to be careful not to get it dirty, so shoes are either taped on the bottoms or wiped off before you get on the set. Anyone who has to walk on the set can't make tracks. Even the stylist and assistants have to take their shoes off, or walk on their knees.

An assistant will test the lighting by holding a meter to my face. Click! The strobes will flash, and

44

he'll know from the reading on the meter whether his light is right. Most photographers will take a Polaroid first. This is to check how everything is going to photograph. The lighting, the set, the clothes—even me.

He'll show the picture to the art director. This person is the one who's creating the ad. The art director knows just the type of picture the client wants. To make sure the photographer gets the right picture for the ad, the art director will sometimes show him a layout. This is kind of a rough sketch of how the finished ad should look. I get to see the layout, too, so I'll know the mood or movement they want. That way, I can help the photographer get the picture he's after.

And the photographer helps me. After he focuses, he'll tell me the area I have to stay in. And while we're shooting, he'll call out instructions to me. Like, "More, more! Let me see those balloons. Too much. We're seeing some clamps. Okay, softer, now. Nice. Good smile. Keep it going. Look right at me, now."

Some photographers talk all the way through. Some don't say much, and others might even yell at you. But you shouldn't take it personally. Sometimes they're the only ones on a shoot who know the effect they're trying to capture. Some photographers will say things like "Okay, now, get giggly," or "Get sulky," when they're not seeing the mood they want from a model. They'll tell you what to do to get the look they're after. So you just have to listen. And play the role.

In the middle of a shooting, or while the film is being changed, the stylist might jump in and put in a pin, smooth out a wrinkle, or hand you a prop to play with. Like these balloons. She might fix your

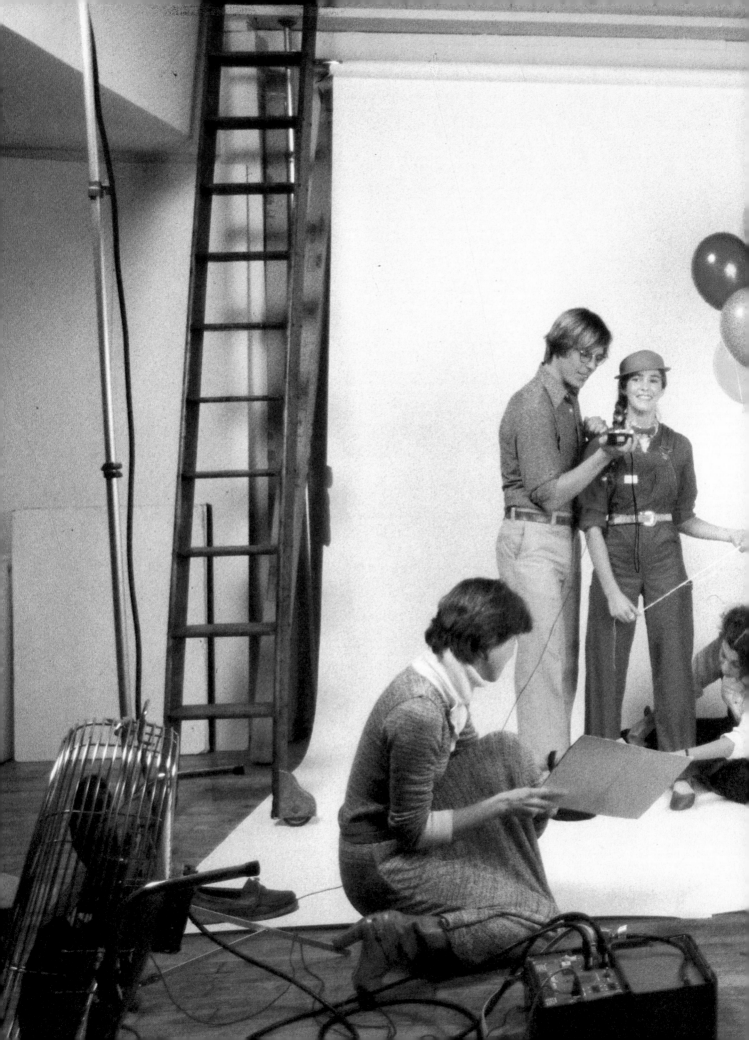

hair so it's smooth, and at other times, they'll turn a fan on so your hair blows.

There's usually music going on, too. That really helps me move. I like working with disco the best (like the Bee Gees). It's nice to have music when you're dancing around, so you don't feel like a complete nut. It's hard jumping and laughing and looking like you're having fun to total silence!

The only object of a shooting is to get the best possible pictures. And everybody works hard to make that happen. Including the model. It might look like she only has to smile and look pretty. But, boy, let me tell you, there are a million things to think about while you're trying to look like you're having a good time. If I move a certain way, will I get a wrinkle? Am I showing the pinnings? Is the collar up? Is my hair hiding anything? Are there pockets? Should I use them? Am I showing what the layout shows? Where's the light? Whoops—did I move out of focus? And, with all those other thoughts going on, do I look natural?

On my way home, I can still hear the photographer saying "A little to the left . . . bend your right knee a touch . . . left hand in your pocket . . . not too hard . . . get your hair off your shoulders . . . straighten up . . . turn a little more to the right . . . now look straight into the camera . . . okay, throw your head back . . . give me your biggest smile now . . . and look natural!"

I think about all the people. I wonder about the pictures. But mostly I think about how tired I am. Modeling may be glamorous, but you sure don't feel glamorous on a crowded subway going home. And you know what else I think about? A biology project, due next week. Back to my other world.

At school: my other life

Getting a booking doesn't mean I get out of school. No such luck. I still have to go like everybody else. Once in a while, if I have a really special shooting, I may have to get out an hour early, but the teachers aren't too crazy about that. So I try not to do it too often. The teachers know I model, and usually they're understanding about it, as long as I make up what I miss in class. Our school day is shorter than most, too (only twenty minutes for lunch), so I have all afternoon free to model.

Of course, that means school starts really early. Usually, I'm up at 7:00 A.M., and on my way by 7:15. The most important thing for me is to get as much sleep as I can. Mom saves me time by having everything ready for me—as usual. And it doesn't take me long to get myself together. I don't put on makeup, so I just have to brush my hair. I get fussed with enough when I'm working. I also don't like to get too dressed up for school. Most of the girls just wear good jeans and blouses. After I gulp down some orange juice and grab a toasted bagel, I'm off.

I go to a public school. A lot of people have asked me why I don't go to a professional children's school. But I grew up here, my friends are here, and I like my school. I like to get involved in school activities, too. Like band. It means getting to school extra early for practice, but I make it. Sometimes, though, I have to miss concerts if I have a booking. Then the band teacher gets mad. But I do, too. I wish I could be both places at the same time.

My best friend, Lauren Gelfand, plays the flute in the band, too. We sit next to each other. We've been friends since the fourth grade, and we've gone to the same school together forever. Before we knew each other, I'd always see her and always want to meet her. Then somebody introduced us, and we've been friends ever since. We're the same type. And we like to do the same things. When we were younger, we'd make each other up and we'd dress up. Now we're into cooking. Every time we get together at each other's house, we always bake something—and eat it, naturally!

Lauren sort of lives close to me. We live on a canal, and I have to walk around it to get to her house. If I had a rowboat, I could just row across, walk half a block, and I'd be there. We like to spend a lot of our free time with each other on the weekends, too. We do everything together, and I know she's someone I can count on. That's important in a friend, besides having a good time with them.

I have a lot of classes with another one of my good friends, Maureen. We always try to sit next to each other. And when we do, we can't help giggling or talking—a lot. Sometimes the teacher separates us, but then we just pass notes. We have this

one class where we all have to grade each other's papers after a test. I feel sort of funny about that if I get a friend's paper. It's hard to mark something wrong when you like the person.

I guess I have a thing about getting A's. My mom tells me to just relax and not worry so much about it, but I do.

At least there are no right or wrong answers in art. We're allowed to do pretty much what we want in that class. It's fun to design things, but I don't think I'll ever be a Rembrandt. I have an older sister, Suzanne, who draws really well. But I guess it doesn't run in the family.

One of my favorite classes is biology. I especially like doing the experiments. If I go on to study archaeology, I know I'll have to take a lot more science courses. And math, too. (I just hope they're not all like geometry.)

Of course, we also goof around a lot in school, too. It's not all work and no play. One of our teachers is a practical joker, so Maureen and I put worms all over the hood of his car. It was a riot, except the only one who got sent to the office was me. Luckily, the principal thought it was pretty funny, so I didn't get into a whole lot of trouble.

One of my biggest problems with being a model is not being able to do sports enough. It seems like every time I go out for one, I get extra busy with a lot of bookings. So I try to pick activities that won't require me being there all the time. Instead of trying out for cheerleading, I volunteer to be manager for the football team. Then I only have to be at the games on Saturday, instead of every practice. Or I keep track of scores for the wrestling team. The hardest thing for me is not being able to be on a team.

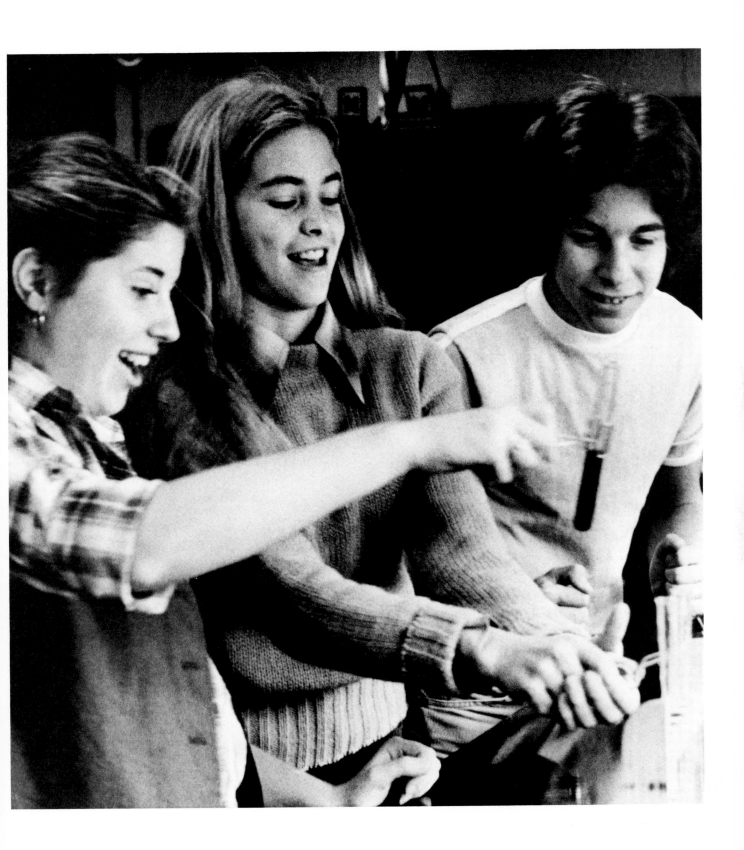

When I have more free time, they let me run with the track team. I love that, and when I work at it, I do pretty well. That's another thing I have in common with Betsy. Track used to be her sport in high school, too. She was voted "Most Athletic," and she felt really silly because a boy wasn't picked. It wouldn't bother me—I just wish I could play enough sports to be "Most Athletic." Whatever I play, I'm determined to win (mom thinks it has to do with my A complex). But I like to really work at sports. I just wish I had more time. My friend Trisha and I tried to get a soccer team together, but I couldn't have been on it, anyway. That really made me feel awful. I'd hate not to be able to make a game, and let everybody down.

It's funny, but when I'm at school I don't think about modeling. But when I'm modeling, I don't think about school. A lot of the kids just hang around after school with nothing to do, and that doesn't sound like a lot of fun to me. So I'm glad I do have places to go.

If I have to miss any school for a whole day's shooting or a location trip, I sometimes run into a few problems. But I try to avoid them in advance. In the beginning of the school year, my mother talks to all my teachers to make them aware of what I do. So that way they're more understanding and will give me my work ahead of time. Sometimes, when I turn the work in, the teacher hasn't gotten as far as he thought, so I could even end up ahead of the class. It can get hectic trying to keep up with school and model at the same time. But as long as I keep good grades, the teachers don't mind. My friends think I'm pretty lucky when I get out of school. That is, until I explain to them that it's double the work for me. So jealousy isn't really a big deal.

If I'm going to be out for a really long time, I may have a tutor. Like the time I went to Japan with my friend Brooke Shields. There we both were studying four hours a day. And Japan was an education in itself. Brooke's mother had us make a list of ten things we learned each day about Japan. When I got back, my teacher saved a day for me to tell the class about it. (Those lists came in handy.) I'm glad my mom agrees that traveling is educational. She thinks it's a good thing that I have the chance to see new places, and get an idea of how other people live.

Because I still don't know what I want to do with my life, grades are important to me. I worry about tests . . . and biology projects . . . and my report card. Mom says I'll live if I get B's. But mostly I get A's. Maybe my lack of time makes me use it better. At least it's teaching me to get as much as I can out of every moment I do have to study. That should prepare me pretty well for college, anyway.

Hurry up and wait

Since my classes end pretty early, I still have time to get into Manhattan for bookings or appointments. Most of the jobs are always in New York, so that makes me an automatic commuter. Mom picks me up at school and packs me off. We traveled in together all the time when I was younger. But now that I've had more experience commuting, I can handle the trip by myself. I kind of like the independence, too. Especially when I have time in between bookings and can look around in all the stores.

Even though mom's not with me, she's still a big help. She'll call the agency and find out where I'm to go, who I should see, and if there's anything special I need to take with me. (Like shoes or bodysuits, or slips, or stockings—whatever.) Then she'll pack up my model bag with my makeup, brushes, and anything else I need. She sometimes even throws in a couple of munchies, too, for those times when things are running later than expected. A chocolate chip cookie tastes even better when you're starving! There are days when you hardly have a minute to eat.

Mom also finds out if I need to bring my portfolio. I don't need to take it to shootings, but if there's a chance that I have an interview afterwards, I should have it. I'll give her my school books, she'll hand me my model bag and portfolio—and I'm off.

If I'm late, I really run for the train. There's only

one that will get me into the city early enough—
and that's the 1:50. If I miss it, I have to wait a
whole hour. I'll buy my ticket on the train to save a
few moments. (It's cheaper to buy it at the station
but then I might miss the train—which means I
might miss a booking, too!) The train is pretty
empty at that time of the afternoon and the con-

ductors all know me. Riding for an hour gives me a good chance to catch up on my schoolwork or if I don't have any, I'll take a quick nap.

When I get to the city, I still have to take a bus or a subway or a cab to my appointment. Take notes, if you ever plan to get around town: You need exact change for a bus, tokens for a subway, and lots of money for a cab. It costs about two bucks just to go around a corner! Sometimes it seems that cabdrivers go down the most crowded streets when you're in a hurry. Of course, every street is crowded—so you need to give yourself plenty of time to get someplace.

Getting there is a lot of hurry-up-and-waiting. And waiting. And waiting. If it's nice out, I like walking—which can often be faster than waiting for a cab or subway. And I can always use the exercise. Subways are the best when you really have to hurry. They can be scary, but they're okay during the day. Mom told me to tuck my hair into my jacket so I'll be less noticeable, and not to look anybody in the eye. I also walk alongside people so I don't look like I'm alone, and I stay away from the edge of the platform!

Traveling around New York is easier than it sounds. All it takes is figuring out which ways get you there the fastest.

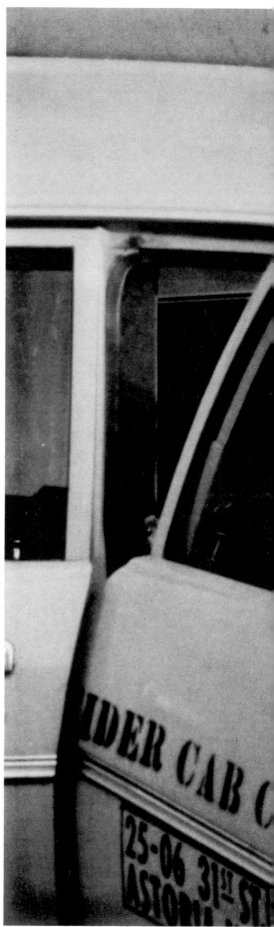

Cattle calls
and go sees

While I'm in the city, I may have an appointment to go to see someone who is considering me for a booking. There are several ways to try out for modeling jobs. But they all involve you going to see the client. In model talk, that's a go-see.

A call might come into Ford's Children's Division for a "preteen 10, all-American girl, about fourteen or fifteen." That means they want to see everybody—and I mean everybody, from every agency—who fits that description. That's what's known as a cattle call. It's a go-see for a cast of thousands. Well, not thousands, actually. Sometimes just a roomful of girls. Just!

Going on a cattle call gives me a good chance to see my modeling friends. But I can't help looking around the room to figure out who might get the job. There are always so many pretty girls at these things. I have to keep reminding myself that it's just a question of who's right for the job.

Before I know it, it's my turn. Front and center, facing the photographer—or stylist—or art director—or editor. Gulp. I show them my portfolio.

72

And smile. And answer questions. And listen. Then someone may snap a Polaroid of me to put with my composite. That's because models are always changing (especially fourteen-year-old ones), and clients need to keep track of the latest "you."

The same things happen on a general go-see. You just *go* (with your portfolio in hand) so the client can *see* you. The difference between a cattle call and a go-see is the number of girls. You could be all by yourself at a go-see. Especially if it's a "request." That means somebody out there has asked to see you—by name. And that's the best.

At some go-sees, the client might ask you to try something on. Then they'll tell you that it's too long, or you're too short, or your hair would have to be cut. The thing to remember is, everybody sees you differently. They'll also pick girls as much for personality as they will for physical appearance. Betsy's always telling me "Remember, people tend to work with people they like." And she's absolutely right. Which is why clients sometimes stick with the model they've used a million times before. A new face can be less important to them than an old friend.

Technically, if you have to try on clothes, you should be booked for a fitting. That's the only time a client can hire a model for just half an hour. Some of the clients who still schedule proper fittings are the pattern companies. They have a seamstress there, and they fit the clothes right to you. They'll shorten the pants, or hems, or take in a seam, or let out a waistline, before the outfit is completely sewn. When it arrives at the shooting, it actually fits, and there's no last-minute pinning for the stylist to do.

Fittings, go-sees, and cattle calls are all things you have to do before you're even in front of a camera. When you're first starting out, you might go on as many as ten go-sees a day. And usually you don't work right away. That's what's called "pounding the pavement." It's not always fun. You're always a little nervous. You're always a little insecure. But you can't think it has anything to do with you personally. A model should think of herself as an image. And that image is either right for the job or not. That's the only way to keep rejection from leading to dejection. At least that's what I

76

keep telling myself. After all, you have to treat it like a business.

After a day of go-sees or bookings, I always phone in to the agency to check if there's anything else to do, or anyone else to see in the city before I catch the train home. If not, I call my mom to let her know I'm coming so she can pick me up at the station. Models spend an awful lot of time dialing from pay phones on the street. You always have to have a million dimes with you. And it's important to keep an eye on your portfolio while you're making a call, or on the subway, bus, train, and taxi. Your pictures are what you've got to sell yourself with, and if you lose them, it's bad news. I can tell you this because it happened to me.

Once, when I was running off the train, I left my portfolio on the seat because I was in such a rush. Boy, was I worried when I realized what I did. But, luckily, a train conductor who knew me found it. He gave it to the station where I get the train every day, and they returned it to me. After that experience, I know it's a good idea to put together two identical portfolios—just in case! Having two also gives the agency a chance to send one out to clients.

If I have no other appointments, I head for Penn Station. It's usually rush hour by then, and the sidewalks are wall-to-wall people. And the station practically swells with commuters. People are all hurrying to catch their trains. Me too. I'm caught up in the fast-moving crowd as I head for home.

A time for fantasy

The real glamour of modeling comes from creating a total fantasy in front of the camera. You can wear things you normally would never wear. You can look whole new ways you normally wouldn't look. By changing your hair and makeup, you can create a completely different image. And it's fun. Like playing make-believe when you were younger. Most of my friends have stopped pretending. But I'm glad I don't have to. With models, it's what we do for a living.

Which is why so many models go into acting. It's just natural. Because when you're in front of a camera to work, you've got to do more than just say "cheese." You've got to communicate something to the camera. A mood . . . or an attitude. That's what comes across in the pictures. Of course, makeup and hair help. And the clothes. But if you can't get into the mood, you'll just look out of place. Like a little kid dressing up.

Sometimes I feel like that on the inside. But then I get into the fantasy of it all and pretend I'm a

whole different person. That's really the most fun of all. I can enter a photographer's studio as myself, and in an hour or so I can be transformed into a sophisticated lady or a romantic bride. In my mind, I create a whole scene to go along with whatever I'm supposed to do—act my age and keep smiling, or pretend I'm older and sexy. That's what makes modeling more magical than any other career. Where else could you play dress-up games in the "real" world *and* get paid for it?

I have to admit that, at fourteen, most of my fantasy shots happen during testing. That's when a photographer and a model get together to experiment with pictures. Both of them constantly need new shots to show to clients, so test sessions are a good way for models and photographers to build up their portfolios.

At first, a model will just have test shots to show. But after she gets some real bookings, she can put in her actual ads, magazine pages, or covers. Because a portfolio is so important to a model's career, the agency will put a warning on it to make sure pictures aren't removed, and offer a reward for returning a lost portfolio.

When a model goes for test shots, nobody charges. But both the photographer and the model get to keep the pictures they want. You need to be patient, though. Sometimes it seems to take forever to select the best pictures from contact sheets or slides, and then to get them from the photographer. You have to remember how busy the photographers are with paying jobs and rush deadlines. Naturally, they get around to the test pictures in their free time. So you should keep calling and reminding them about your pictures. Some models

get discouraged and give up doing test shots. But they shouldn't. Testing is really important all through a model's career if she wants to keep her portfolio up to date, and show as many different looks of herself as she possibly can.

When you start out, the pictures in your portfolio can be pretty basic—just head shots, smiles, profiles, and full-length shots. But then, through testing, you can experiment with all sorts of looks you might not get a chance to show. And you can work on expanding your image. For instance, most of my jobs now just call for me to be me. Well, me·as a normal fourteen-year-old. Sometimes I have to be a tomboy, sometimes I'm in prom dresses. And I've just got to smile a lot and look natural. I must have my fourteen-year-old act down pat because right now I'm booked to be exactly what I am—"the girl next door." But I know my portfolio has to change and grow as I change and grow. And when I do test shots, I can be anything. Even asleep.

Testing also gives you a chance to try out the latest fashion trends in makeup and hair looks, and add them to your portfolio. Usually the photographer will have a certain effect in mind for the shots—a special lighting, or set, or technique to try. A model can help create the fantasy with special makeup and clothes. It's the two of you working together to create the image.

I was lucky to test with Betsy. She showed me a lot about changing my looks. Some photographers don't know as much about makeup and hair tricks. Betsy does, because as a model she's had to learn. And she really helped me add a lot of super pictures to my portfolio.

There's another reason I'm glad I went when Betsy called Claudia for any young models who wanted to test. One of the test shots wound up in the first issue of *Life!* Another one got into the first issue of *Look!* A lot of the pictures in this book are the result of testing, too. So a model can never think that testing isn't the real thing. You never know who might see the pictures.

To give me lots of different images, we did a whole series of fantasy shots. And the most important effect Betsy was after in all of them was creating a mood. Which meant lighting, clothes, and locations were all important. She started with different outfits that suggested completely different moods. They were almost like costumes. We went to this fantastic antique clothes place, Gene London Associates, where you can rent all sorts of beautiful, unusual outfits. Like a real leopard coat and a satin antique clown outfit. And velvet dresses, lacy jackets, and romantic sequin caps. It was like raiding a wonderful trunk to play dress-up.

The next step was to create the right face for

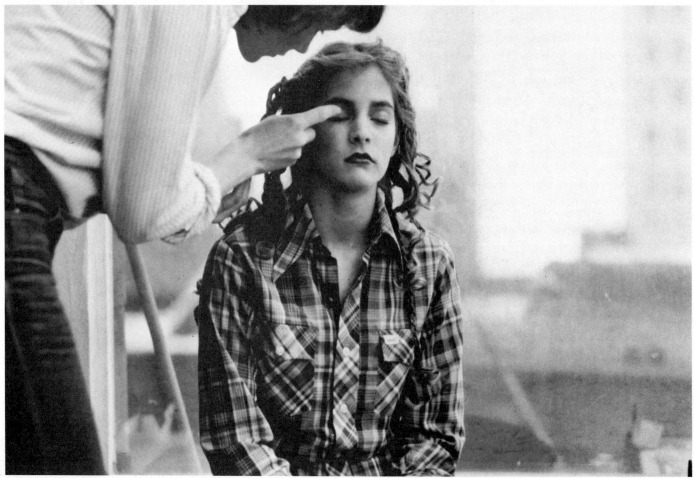

each mood. Betsy's a genius with makeup. For my *Leopard Lady* look, she made me look exotic, right down to my long, red nails. (Great *fakes*—and a lot of models get away with them for closeup hand and nail shots.) There's no way my own nails could ever get that long. Anyhow, they'd get in the way of everything I do. Imagine them at school! But they are kind of fun for a shooting. They made me feel really feminine and sophisticated.

We worked all morning creating a new me. Betsy contoured my face with makeup, dark just under the cheekbones. Then she made my eyes very dark and dramatic by rimming them with black eyeliner.

Before we got into hair, it was time out for a turkey sandwich. Even Leopard Ladies have to eat. (Which reminds me to tell you, they stop for lunch at real shootings, too.)

Then Betsy unbraided my hair, gave me bright red lips to match my bright red nails—and suddenly, I looked like a whole different person.

It's all in the know-how. Betsy says you can take most anyone and make them into a fantasy. Well, she can, anyway. But, really, if you saw some models on the street without any makeup at all, you wouldn't even recognize them. Most people think models have to be exceptionally beautiful, but it's not true. The most important thing is bone structure and a little magic with makeup.

For the series of test shots in this chapter, Betsy transformed me completely each time. I was everything from a thirties movie star to an old-fashioned clown. A model has to learn that just because she's in front of the camera, it doesn't mean that people are going to recognize her.

To show that I wasn't too young to do more sophisticated fashion shots, Betsy did a few of me in silk pajamas. Just call me *China Girl*. I tried to use my most worldly stare. And I think my hair on top of my head helped me to look a little older, too.

I still have to show that I can be a normal kid, too. Remember—versatility. So we did a funky *Tomboy*. At least I didn't have to worry about getting dirty in these clothes. I even climbed an apple tree for some of the shots.

We shot the *Country Girl* look after a lot of driving around, looking for the "perfect" location. What we finally found was cold, hard ground for me to sit on—and biting mosquitoes. And we only had time to take two shots before the sun set. But you've got to be able to just shut all those things out and concentrate on the mood the photographer wants. That's what's called "faking it."

The *Sailor* shot was taken that same day, too. We were working out of a van, and I kept changing clothes—and moods. Naturally, you feel differently in a sailor suit than you do holding a bunch of

90

flowers. And that comes across in your expression—hopefully.

Testing helps me work on my attitudes. A model has to be able to show any feeling the photographer wants. You can't be awkward, or giggle, or say "I can't do that." Not if you want to work. You have to feel into the clothes, as well as fill into them. Which means you have to just be relaxed, confident, and responsive. I'm working on creating attitudes now (even in the mirror at home). Sometimes I can see a completely different me. If I tilt my head down and just stare straight ahead, like I did for the shot with the black cat, I can look much, much older. I think it has to do with the expression you put in your eyes. I keep practicing that look—because I know I can't get away with being fourteen forever.

For my *Pierrot* shot, the white-face makeup did a pretty good job of disguising me. It's the hardest stuff to work with. The black eyeliner and mascara kept smearing into it. But this turned out to be one of Betsy's favorite shots.

The day we did the bathing-suit shots I was really cold. (Betsy said I was a grouch, and told me to just keep thinking warm and beautiful thoughts.) The wind blowing my hair helped me to feel romantic. It's another look I don't get to use very often as a fourteen-year-old.

Sometimes, to create the right mood, you don't even have to face the camera. One of the best of these shots turned out to be the one with me walking away from the camera into the ocean.

When you're shooting, everything will suggest the right expression to you: the lighting, the location, the clothes—and the photographer. Being *The Bride* was easy. Betsy wanted to shoot into the

91

mirror, so I could see what I was doing. That's very rare. Usually, you don't get to watch yourself work. It can get pretty distracting. What I hope the picture doesn't show is that I had to catch a train home, and we were so rushed, we only had time to shoot one roll of film.

Sometimes you have to show a wide range of moods for just one outfit. That's the hardest work. We spent two hours on the shots of me in the white satin dress (our *Sunset* pictures). Can you imagine thinking up enough different expressions to last two hours? But if the photographer just keeps shooting away, you have to. You can play off different accessories, like an umbrella or a jacket. Or you can create your own fantasy story in your imagination as you go along. Or you can just listen to the photographer. Betsy kept saying "Wow! What light! You look just fantastic!" And that really helped me to feel beautiful. It's amazing how light can change the mood of a photograph. It changes your mood, too—and your looks. Sometimes Betsy would run up from behind her camera and brush my hair a new way. And that would give me another new look.

You learn to work with clothes this way. It's almost a kind of communication between what you're wearing and how you're feeling. If you have to make something look great for two hours, you figure out how to get the most out of it. A lot of the clothes aren't the greatest, either. You also have to feel beautiful in a baggy $1.98 outfit. Or make something you feel ridiculous in look good. But it all helps you to be a better model. Whether it's for testing—or for real.

Doing doubles

Bookings for catalogue work are about as far away from fantasy test shots as you can get. For one thing, the client cares about showing the clothes as clearly as possible—every button, pocket, and stitch. Plus, you usually have a lot of different outfits to shoot during the booking, so you've really got to work fast. Because you get paid by the hour (not by the number of outfits), it's a lot more work for the same pay. I guess that's why they call catalogue work the "meat and potatoes" of the business. It's not the most glamorous kind of work, but even the most glamorous models do it.

At these bookings, you may be working with a whole group of people, or there might be just one other model to share the camera with. That's what's known as doing doubles. I like it when there's another model around for catalogue shoots. Especially if she's someone I've worked with a lot. You can become pretty good friends with other models you're booked with over and over again. There's not as much jealousy going on as you'd think, and a lot to be learned.

It's fun to run into somebody you haven't seen in a while at a shooting. The minute we meet in the dressing room, we start gossiping like crazy. We catch up on what we've each been doing: who we've worked with lately, what location trips we've been on, stuff like that. But it's not all shoptalk, either. You've got to find out the important things, too. Like what's going on at each other's schools and who's got a crush on who. The funny thing is, after all our talking, when the photographer says "Pretend you're talking together," we may run out

of things to say. So we whisper a lot of "Blah, blah, blah" into each other's ears. Or we tell jokes and usually crack everybody up. If they want us to look like we're having a good time—we do!

Of course, it's hard to have too good a time when you're stuck standing on phone books, and with a bounce board held at your waists. These are things the shots never show. The bounce board is used to fill in the light so it is even and pretty, and direct it at what's being shot. In this case, it's going to be an ad for shirts, so they really have to show up. Some-

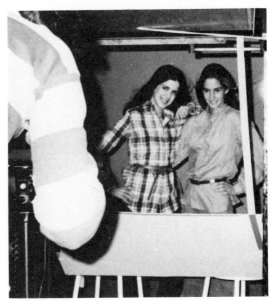

times, for beauty closeups, they want all the light to go directly to your face, so you might have one of these bounce boards held right at your neck.

The shirts were just part of the many clothes we shot at this catalogue booking. It turned out we did three different outfits in one hour. (By the way, you rarely get to keep the clothes.) For each new outfit we had to get pinned and styled all over again. And we had to be extra careful not to get any wrinkles. They're even more worried about wrinkles at these shoots. Can you imagine—one photographer used to nail shoes to the set when he was doing catalogues with children. (Before their feet were in them, of course.) That way, the models couldn't move. For every new look, it's good if you change your hair a little, too. You have to move fast, and it's usually a long day's shoot.

You don't always do doubles with models you know—or, for that matter, even with models your own age. When I was younger, I worked with a lot of adult models for mother/daughter shots. And now that I'm getting older, I sometimes work with younger kids. I'm not the "mother" yet—more like the big sister. But it's fun. I feel really experienced around the younger ones. On this shoot, I was the one telling them to think warm thoughts. It was freezing out, and we had to pretend it was summer. When you're used to that, all you concentrate on is the shot. But sometimes the only thing little kids want to know is if they're done yet!

Sometimes your partner can be a male model, too. I worked with boys when I was younger, but it's more interesting now. There's a difference between being on set with an eight-year-old kid and an eighteen-year-old boy. The first time I ever worked with a guy my own age, the photographer

wanted us to kiss. It wouldn't have been that bad, but it was kind of embarrassing since I had never met him before. The hardest thing to do, though, is just stare into each other's eyes while the photographer shoots two rolls of film. You end up looking at each other's foreheads to keep from going cross-eyed or breaking into hysterics. Usually, when you start out, you stand about two feet apart and you're a little shy. But then you relax a little and get into it and start clowning around. By the end of the day, you know everything about each other. It's like you're old friends.

I'm finding out that working with male models can definitely help your social life. That's why a lot of models date—doing a shooting with someone

can make you instant friends. It's a good thing, too. Betsy told me that some of the girls sit home by the phone without dates. Guys just don't ask them out because they think a model would never go out with an "ordinary" person. (Silly, huh?) So, they go out with male models. The age-old rumor that most of them are gay just isn't so. You can ask the Women's Division!

After a shooting, all the pictures that were taken are shown on a contact sheet. That picks up every click of the camera—almost like a filmstrip. The client will look at the contacts through a magnifying glass (or loop), and select the shots to be blown up. Sometimes, they'll select several alternates and wait to see what they look like as prints before they make the final decision for the ad. Then the final choice is made up, retouched (if necessary), and put into the artist's layout. And you've got an ad.

Child models usually get a lot of catalogue work. It can be for pattern companies, or stores, or clothing manufacturers. Yup—these are me—through the years. But I've been lucky enough to do all kinds of work, from fashion layouts in magazines to lots of family ads. It's all part of growing up as a model.

Hair and makeup tricks

When you're modeling lots of different outfits during a booking, your hair and makeup looks have to change, too. Some days you could start out wearing a prom dress, and end up in a ski jacket. And you have to create the right face and hair styles for each one. Knowing lots of tricks to make yourself over—quickly—in the middle of a shooting is part of being professional. Nobody likes to waste time while the model sits there wondering how she should fix her hair or her face. You just have to know what you're doing, and then do it as fast as you can.

My favorite way to wear my hair when I'm just being me is to wrap an elastic headband around a ponytail. This is good for sports—it keeps my hair out of my face. The elastic headband looks pretty, and it also keeps the ends from breaking. All my long-haired friends know this trick.

I usually just go to a shooting with clean, natural hair. Because you never know what look they're going to want until you get there. For instant curl, most photographers have electric rollers in their

dressing rooms. For even faster curls or frizz, most hairstylists will use a curling iron or crimper. But both of these can really dry your hair out, so you've got to keep using a good conditioner on your hair all the time.

So that I can go to a shooting with the right amount of curl in my hair, I try to find out from the agency ahead of time what look the client is going to want. I'll even sleep on soft rollers the night before if I have to. Then I can just brush my hair out when I get there. I bend over, brush it through, then flip it back. This gives it instant body, and my hair's ready for anything.

It's important to learn how to create the latest styles on yourself. It takes practice. And knowing what your hair will and will not do. Does it hold a curl? Is it fuller looking if it's layered? Is it more manageable right after you wash it, or a day later? You can only find these things out by experimenting with your own hair.

Now that there are so many ways to change long hair around, models can let their hair grow. As long as they know what to do with it. Betsy told me that just a few years ago, you couldn't have really long hair. It had to stop at your shoulders to show the collars. Braids and twists hadn't come in yet, so there were few ways to make long hair look any shorter. Clients would ask you to cut it, or they might not book you. I'm glad that's changed. Lauren and I are having a contest to see whose hair can grow down to their rear end first. I figure I better do it now, or I'll never have another chance.

Betsy's taught me a lot of different things to do with my hair so I don't have to have just one long look. By using different kinds of curling techniques, it can go from long and natural to bouncy and

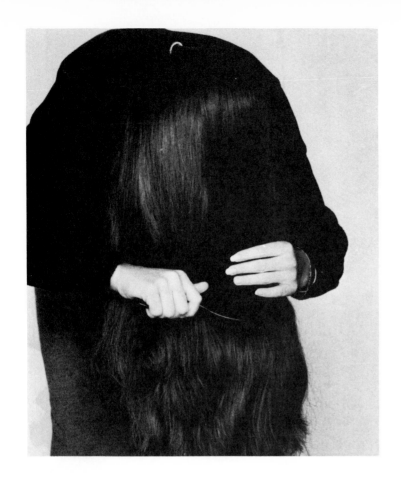

shorter, to neatly rolled around my head. It's fun to play around with all the looks.

To just let it go straight and soft, I have to brush it out while I'm blowing it dry. My hair has a little bit of natural wave to it, and this takes some of that out. It would never go straight if I just let it dry by itself. For a natural look, I can just brush it out straight (as long as it has plenty of shine), or braid a few strands at one side, or braid both sides, bring them around to the back, and tuck in special sparklies. This gives me sort of a romantic, Juliet look. The best makeup for these kinds of natural hairstyles is very sheer and light. Betsy used a pale base to take the yellow out of my skin tones. Then she used a see-through gel instead of a powder for a blush. That gives color without covering up your skin with layers of makeup. She gave me a light

SOFT AND NATURAL

121

dusting of baby powder on top of everything, so I'd look even paler. To make my eyes look big (but natural), there's a light blue line right on the inside rim of my lower lashes, and a darker blue line underneath the lashes. The shine on my lids comes from a clear gel. I'll tell you a secret—it's called "Eight Hour Cream," and lots of models use it. I put it around the corners of my eyes every night before I go to bed. I put it over my lipstick, too, and then touch it to my cheekbones. The extra little shine really gives a healthy glow. To finish off this look—lots and lots of mascara.

GLAMOUR GIRL

For a real glamour-girl effect, I braid my hair all over when it's wet, then roll the braids into pin curls. That's a lot easier than winding up a pin curl with hair this long. For a more exciting makeup look to go with the hair, Betsy just used a black liner around my eyes, and no mascara this time. She kept my face pale and my lips bright. This is to make the eyes and lips the most important focal points.

If I use perm rod curlers (they're smaller than rollers), I end up with little girl curls. With lots of bounce—and I mean lots! Since this gives me a really young look, I hardly have any makeup on at all. Just a little blush, mascara, and baby powder to make me look delicate. There's just a little bit of color on my lips, so they don't wash out under the lights. That's one thing you have to remember when you're putting on makeup for a shooting. It has to be a little obvious, or it won't show up at all.

LITTLE GIRL CURLS

A way to get less waves but more frizz is to braid your hair, then curl just the ends of the braid. This is kind of a sophisticated look, so Betsy gave me the full makeup treatment. She outlined my eyes in dark colors so they'd look big and mysterious. Then even my eyelashes and eyebrows got into the act. Brushing my eyebrows straight up gave my face a completely different look. And this time she curled my lashes so they'd look longer. Then she shaded my nose down the sides with a darker color to give it a sculpture shape, and she shaded the hollows of my cheeks to make my cheekbones look more prominent. Finally, bright red lipstick tops off everything else that's going on.

THE FRIZZ

Pipe-cleaner coils give me the wildest combination of waves, frizz, and curls. I just bend a pipe cleaner in half and wrap a small strand of hair back and forth between each side. Sort of like weaving the hair. Then I just twist the ends together, and it stays in. But I warn you—you have to take your time and have a lot of patience to do this. Especially when taking them out. It's a great look for disco clothes, though. After I brush it out (just *slightly*), I put pipe cleaners back in. But this time, they're sparkly gold ones that I got at a party decorations store. Just wrap a few in around small strands of curls, and your hair is dressed up. For a special nighttime makeup look, I add even more glitter. Like a frosted eye shadow and lots of gloss over my lipstick for extra shine. Betsy used a brighter blusher with dark shading in the hollows. And then a couple coats of mascara, and I'm ready to go disco.

DISCO GLITTER

When I do my own makeup, I keep it really basic. A little base to even out my skin tone and cover up my scars. I got one from running into a metal bar once at a playground. That left me with a scar near my hairline. Then I've got two more from falling against a coffee table. I'm always banging into something. See? You can be a klutz and still be a model! As long as you're not clumsy in front of the cameras. You don't have to be perfect, either. If you have something you really hate about yourself, don't waste time worrying about it. Think of ways to cover up what bothers you and make the most of what you have. I hate my ears. No kidding, they're pointy at the top, just like Spock on "Star Trek." So I try to avoid hairstyles that show them.

Makeup doesn't help my ears, but it does improve everything else. After I put on a base color, I use a pink blush to make me look extra healthy and to contour my cheekbones so they show up better. Betsy showed me how to smile at myself in the mirror to figure out where to put the blush for contouring. You put it right where your cheeks puff up when you smile. Then you can also suck your cheeks in and put a darker color right in the hollows. This really defines the shape of your face, but it tends to give you an older look. So I normally don't use the darker contouring to look natural.

Then I put some mascara on two or three times to make my eyes look bigger. You have to do this carefully. If you smudge it, you'll have to start all over again with base. As a last touch, I use just a little lip gloss for shine. All this makeup, and I just have a natural, unmadeup look. If I had to look like I was really wearing makeup (for a cosmetic ad, for instance), you should see how much stuff I'd have to put on my face.

It's fun to change your image. By knowing the tricks, you can really look like a whole different person.

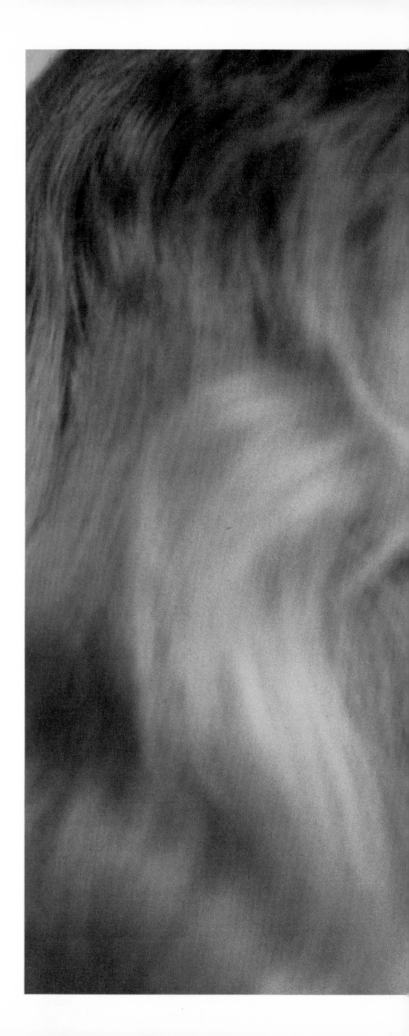

THE FRIZZ

LITTLE GIRL CURLS

GLAMOUR GIRL

DISCO GLITTER

As a younger model, you just have to have a very natural look. But as you start doing different situations—from school to date shots, for instance—you need to know how to create the right image.

It's important for both makeup and hair looks to go together. You wouldn't mix dramatic disco makeup with natural-looking hair. The wilder the style, the more emphasis you have to put on your face. On the other hand, for really sporty hair looks, less makeup is better. So they both have to look right with each other. Of course, for days when your face has a case of the uglies, hair is sometimes better to hide behind!

Take two: T.V. commercials

It's always a good idea to find out exactly what look to walk in with when you're trying out for a TV commercial. These people really typecast, and if they're looking for a frizzy-haired girl, they want to see a frizzy-haired girl. It's no use to stand there with straight hair and explain about pipe cleaners. They'll just give the job to the next frizzy-haired girl who walks in.

I always ask exactly what kind of type and what kind of "character" they want. Should I be a girl-next-door, or intellectual and shy, or a sporty jock? Then, from the moment I walk in, I try to act the part. Because, in most cases, making a commercial is more than just looking good. It's acting.

Getting a commercial is a little more involved than just showing your portfolio at a go-see. Usually, the casting director wants to see what you look like—on film. (If you have lines, they have to hear how your voice records, too.) So you go to a video session. When you get there, somebody might hand you a script to read over for a few minutes while you're waiting. Then you audition in front of the camera. You have to stand on a certain line, state

your name and agency—and you're on! You might have to read your lines, or just talk to the director, or even sing and dance. What they're looking for is how animated you are once the cameras roll. It's not the time to freeze. You've got to let your personality come through. And—act natural.

Some days can get very confusing when TV and print go-sees come in at the same time. Luckily, my TV manager and Claudia try to arrange my schedule so I can get to both. Even if it means I have to do a quick switch from looking older for a print go-see, and younger for a commercial call.

What I did at this audition must have worked, because I got the job. (Maybe my braids had something to do with it.) It was for Avon, and I was the daughter. My part didn't come in until the last few seconds of it. But in order to get it just the way they wanted it, we were shooting until 2:00 in the morning. I was glad my mom was with me on this job because it went on so late that they had to put us up for the night in a hotel. That's show biz!

Making a commercial is totally different than a print shooting. You have a script, there's a set, and you have about a million people on the crew all standing around watching you. There are grips, electricians, sound technicians, script people, set designers, set decorators, hairdressers, makeup artists, stylists, cameramen, directors, and lots of assistants. And it takes much longer, too. Some days you could go about fourteen hours. And after about forty tries (they're called "takes"), you may have the start of one thirty-second commercial!

Why do you have to do it so many times? Well, a million things can go wrong while you're filming. Once, on about the eleventh take of an orange juice commercial, I turned to smile, burst out

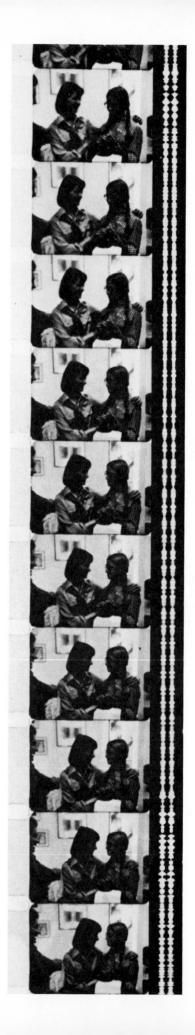

laughing, and spat orange juice all over the place. Pass another glass of orange juice, please! Yes—you do have to drink a glass for every take.

Or the director might decide he wants to try the same scene from different angles. I actually had braces put on my teeth for a yogurt commercial. Then they decided not to use any of the closeups. Of course, the braces were the removable kind.

In spite of the hard work, I really like to do commercials. It's fun because it's so different from photographic modeling. You're not always the center of the camera's attention. But if your face gets on camera at all, you get residuals. Once, filming a marathon race, I was in the middle of a hundred people on bikes. Nobody could really tell I was in that commercial—except me. My muscles hurt for days after filming that one.

I've been lucky so far and gotten in a lot of commercials. For Avon, Dannon Yogurt, Kool-Aid, One A Day, Sunkist, Cheez-Its, Mellow Roast Coffee, Hamilton Beach, Manufacturers Hanover Trust, Pepsi, Paper Mate, and Tupperware. It does give me a funny tingle to be watching TV—and suddenly see myself.

137

Weekend: time off

Even though mom doesn't come on jobs with me anymore, we still do things together when I have free time. That's usually the weekends. And am I glad when Saturday comes. It's my day to sleep late—and I do!

When I finally get up, I jump into the shower and start my "beauty routine." It's simple and basic, but like Betsy says, once you get used to it, it becomes a habit.

I have to take care of my skin, my hair, and my whole body. That begins with a good wake-up shower. (Hot water first, then rinse in cool.) I wash my hair at the same time, and the cold rinse makes it shine. To keep my hair in good condition for the camera, I wash it every other day. Mostly at night, because it takes so long to dry.

With all the modeling makeup and grime from the city, I have to take extra care of my face now, too. Since I probably put more makeup on my face than most girls my age, I need to do more than just wash it to keep my skin in shape. And, naturally,

clear skin is important—there's no hiding pimples from the camera. So first I wash with soap and water. Then I dab on astringent to close the pores. It's good for oily places, like around my nose and on my forehead. It tingles, but it makes my face feel really clean. As a last step, I use a light moisturizing cream. At my age, I normally wouldn't need this. But working under lights and wearing a lot of makeup could dry my skin out. And I don't want to take any chances. When the camera comes in close, your skin has got to be in perfect shape.

Teeth get the next treatment. Fortunately, I didn't need braces (except for that commercial!), but with all the smiling I have to do, I want my teeth to look really white.

I don't like to spend time fixing my hair on weekends (that's for work). If I just braid it while it's still wet from washing, it goes into great waves later.

On Saturdays, I try to do my exercises. They're sort of a combination of things I learned in gym class and dance classes. A couple of calisthenics, a little gymnastics, some ballet, and even some yoga. Whatever I'm into at the moment. Right now, I love gymnastics. If I keep practicing, I might even learn to do it right.

On Saturday afternoons, I go to a local theatre class. We do all sorts of things, from dance routines, to skits, to singing. It helps me to be more expressive as a model, and it's gotten me over my shyness a little bit, too. You either need confidence to be a good model—or you need to be able to act like you're confident. With me, it's still all acting. I can use my training in this class for TV commercials, too. I needed extra speech lessons to help me get rid of my accent. It's not really bad, but it used to sound more New York-y than all-American.

Now I'm working more on my tone, so I don't sound squeaky when I get excited.

My best friend, Lauren, is in the class too, so we have lots of fun. Usually, I don't like to talk too much about my modeling experiences to kids at school. They might think I'm bragging or something. But they're always finding my pictures and telling me about them.

After class you can find me pigging out at the local pizza parlor—and going for a cone for dessert. Who says all models diet? Later, my next-door neighbor and I might give a living-room concert. I really like to play the flute. More than just in

band. Mom used to rent a flute for me. But then, when I won a contest, I bought my own silver flute. That was the first big thing I ever bought myself with my modeling money.

Saturday nights I usually go places with a bunch of friends. We might play at the arcade, go to the movies, or just hang out at the beach. Nobody's dating seriously yet. But if a boy calls you often enough on the phone, everyone says you're going together. My mom thinks that's funny. I've had a few crushes, but I still feel like just one of the gang when we all go out together.

When I get home, I like to sneak a late-night

yogurt from the fridge. Then I go to sleep. If you're wondering why that poster's on the wall, it's because I got to meet Farrah Fawcett when I was in France. She autographed it, so my mom hung it up. The best part was—I'm almost as tall as she is!

On Sundays, if I don't have anything special to do (except homework), I sleep even later. But I like to get out and do stuff on Sunday. Like round up some friends and go play in the park. One time, Betsy, her brothers, and I spent the whole day selling his dog's puppies. They were so cute, I felt like keeping them all—but my mom wasn't too crazy about that idea. Partly because we already have a cat. We found her on the street, looking lonely and lost. Mom and I couldn't resist. Everybody kept saying "What a pretty cat," so we call her Pretty.

The best thing about weekends is that I can be outdoors. We live in a suburb that's right on the beach. There are boardwalks and everything. It's neat—especially all during the summer. We practically spend all day there because there's so much to do. We also have tennis courts by the school that we can use, and ice-skating rinks. Right now, I keep hoping they'll turn them into roller rinks. I don't know how great I'd be at that, but I am pretty good on a skateboard. I also love to play tennis, ride horses, and ski whenever I get the chance. Sports really keep me limber for modeling. Your body's got to be able to move in any direction. You might have to hold a really uncomfortable position. And you need your muscles to cooperate.

One good way to build up your leg muscles is by bike riding. And we do a lot of that where I live. Almost everybody has a bike. We get around that way—even in the winter. And in the summer, we're on our bikes all day.

Sundays give mom and I a good chance to spend some time together. It's fun to cook a big breakfast and just sit around and talk. I do the cooking. Mom doesn't eat anything. She's always on a diet—unless she finds my chocolate chip cookies! We can talk the whole morning away. And we talk about *everything*—teachers, boys, funny modeling stories. I can tell her anything. (And I usually do, too.)

Some kids my age drink beer and smoke pot, or try it out, mostly. The people I'm close to haven't gone into drugs or smoking or drinking. Somebody I knew took a lot of drugs and got addicted and it sort of scared me. I don't really want to try it. Mom and I don't just talk about heavy stuff, though. We laugh a lot. She's as crazy as I am!

My mom and I are like best friends as well as mother and daughter. I think that's good. What really made us close was when we used to go into the city all the time together for my modeling assignments. And even though she stays home now, I still tell her everything that happens. We're also close because I'm like an only child. My two older sisters have grown up and moved away. We're all five years apart and all look very different. I'm the youngest one. Suzanne is next. She lives upstate. She's the one who's really talented in art and she also plays the piano and the guitar. Joanne is the oldest and very dark. She works for an insurance company in California. I hope I get a job out there modeling, so I can go out and visit her. I really miss her.

My grandfather on my father's side came from Austria, so I'm part German. My grandmother used to be a model in the twenties. She was really tall for that time—5′ 8″ or 9″. The only tall one in the family! On my mother's side, my grandparents

150

came from Russia and Poland. They lived near us, and when I was little, we saw a lot of them until they died a few years ago. Their parents died in Europe in the war.

My parents are divorced, and my father doesn't live in New York. He's a pilot and he has his own flying service. He flies horse people mostly—jockeys and trainers to tracks like Saratoga. He loves sports, too. He's an outdoorsman. He plays tennis and paddle ball. When he was sixteen he began ski jumping, but a few years ago the engine of his plane froze over Rhode Island and he had to crash-land in a marsh, barely missing a house. His legs were in casts for three years. So he doesn't ski jump anymore, but now he's been asked to be an adviser on ski jumping for the Olympics.

I've always been scared of flying, but not just because of this. I just don't like it. But I do like to go visit my dad. We're like friends, too. He always plans special things for us to do together. We've gone on some really great skiing trips. Even just going to visit him in Florida is like a super vacation.

I don't feel like I live in a broken home or anything. It's just sort of spread out.

On location in Saint Croix

Even though I hate to fly, going on location for a booking is something I'd never pass up. It's the best! If you're lucky enough to get a trip, you get to see exciting places and go with exciting people—all expenses paid. On top of that, you even get paid for it. Of course, you have to work, too. You can't goof off all that much. Everybody's just as serious about getting good shots as they are inside a photographer's studio.

Magazines (or advertisers, or catalogue companies) shoot on location because they have to work so many months ahead of time. And the weather or the background has to look like the right season. They've got to shoot bathing suits in the middle of winter and ski clothes at the end of the summer to make their deadlines. That means you could literally be doing Christmas in July. It's kind of hard to get into the spirit, but clients have their own schedules, and they have nothing to do with the month it is on the calendar.

154

When you go on a location trip, you work with a whole team of people. An editor, art director, photographer, and usually other models. Sometimes writers, agency people, and clients go along, too. There can also be hairstylists and makeup artists. You have to create the pages of a magazine or the ad wherever you go. Sometimes there's a location van along if you're traveling out to the middle of nowhere. (Or even to the middle of New York. Central Park is a location everybody uses if they want trees in the shot.) Inside a van it's just like a model's dressing room, with lighted makeup mirrors, and places to keep all the clothes and accessories. It's convenient for changing, so you don't have to hide in the bushes. But I've had to do that, too. And it's not a lot of fun. Usually, you're freezing and afraid of being seen. You just have to throw everything on in a hurry. Even location shootings have a tight time schedule, so anything that saves time is important.

I went on a location trip to St. Croix for *Seventeen*. And it was really fun. It was a full week of being in the sun and playing all my favorite sports. For the kind of pictures they wanted, I got to play tennis, soccer, volleyball—even baseball. Plus, we had to swim, dive, and jog on the beach.

You never know when you're going to be called upon to use sports in modeling. You could easily miss a trip because you don't know how to ski or swim. And you shouldn't fake it. I know a girl who went all the way to Aspen, Colorado, and told the photographer she could ski. When she got on the mountain, she was scared to death. You've got to look like you know what you're doing. I've seen some models who didn't know how to hold a tennis racquet drive photographers crazy. They have to keep stopping the shooting to say "No! Like this!" If you feel awkward as a model, you're going to look awkward. People will actually send in letters saying "That girl can't play tennis."

My athletic abilities really came in handy on the *Seventeen* trip. Even though, the first day there, I stepped on about a million sea urchins when my flipper fell off while I was snorkeling. I got needles stuck all over my feet, and scrapes all over my legs from the coral. The next day we had to shoot all the running up and down the beach shots. It wasn't so easy to smile—or run.

There were five other models on the trip, and we all became good friends. If some of us weren't in a particular picture, we could go off and swim, or play games, or just talk. So it was like being with a bunch of friends on vacation. I guess a location trip could be terrible if people didn't get along. There you are, stuck someplace with a bunch of strange people. It just works out better if everybody's cooperative, even-tempered, and helpful.

I have to admit, I felt a little bit like Cinderella. We flew down on a big private plane. And everything was the best all the way. Here I was working

with the cream of the crop—fashion editors, a makeup artist, hairstylist, and photographer. You can really learn a lot from these people. They even taught me how to eat escargots (snails) when we all went out to dinner together. I never would have done that at home!

If you go on location for a magazine, you get paid at the editorial rate. That's less by the day than you get for other clients. But that's what magazines pay because it's such good exposure. As a model gets seen more and more on the editorial pages of magazines, more and more people will call to book her at the full rate. Which can be, tops for kids, $75 an hour, or $600 for a day rate. But the trip was all so much fun, I almost didn't care if I got paid or not.

Cover story:
trying out

The most exciting thing a model can get from magazine work is a cover. Imagine walking by a newsstand, and seeing your face all over the place! It really gives a big boost to anybody's ego and it can be very important to a model's career. When you think about how many models there are, the number that have been cover girls is really a very small percentage. Betsy's been on twelve so far. But being a top model doesn't automatically mean you'll be on a magazine cover. Some of the most famous models haven't been, and some unknowns have. The editors have to take a lot of different things into consideration. The model has to look like the image of the magazine, and the picture has to look right for that particular issue. If your picture's not picked, it doesn't necessarily mean it's not good. It just may not go with the issue for that month.

Most of the time, you have to try out for a cover. And a few other models could be trying out right along with you. It's an exciting, scary experience because you know when you go in that it could be you on the next cover. Even the people at the magazine don't know which girl they want for sure. It all depends on the pictures.

Seventeen called me in for a cover try because somebody there saw Betsy's test picture of me with Brooke in *Life* magazine. They were doing a cover try with two models who had been on the location trip that was going to be featured in that particular issue. Since I hadn't been on that trip, I felt lucky to be asked to try out.

There was a makeup artist and a hairdresser, and they changed each of us over about three or four times. I could watch as the other girls were in front of the camera—and they could watch me. But I think each of us was concentrating on what we were doing, and not thinking too much about the competition. I guess we were all a little nervous.

The photographer asked me to make every funny face I could think of—just to loosen up. So I kept changing faces like crazy to give them a lot to pick from. I couldn't help thinking how great it would be to have my first cover. It was even more important to me because I had always sort of looked up to the models in *Seventeen* while I was growing up (Betsy included). And now, I had the chance to be a *Seventeen* cover girl, too!

I didn't know if I got the cover or not for what seemed like the longest time. Right before I went on the location trip, I was at *Seventeen* for a fitting. Nobody said anything at first. And then, when I was trying something on, somebody walked in and said "Guess what?"

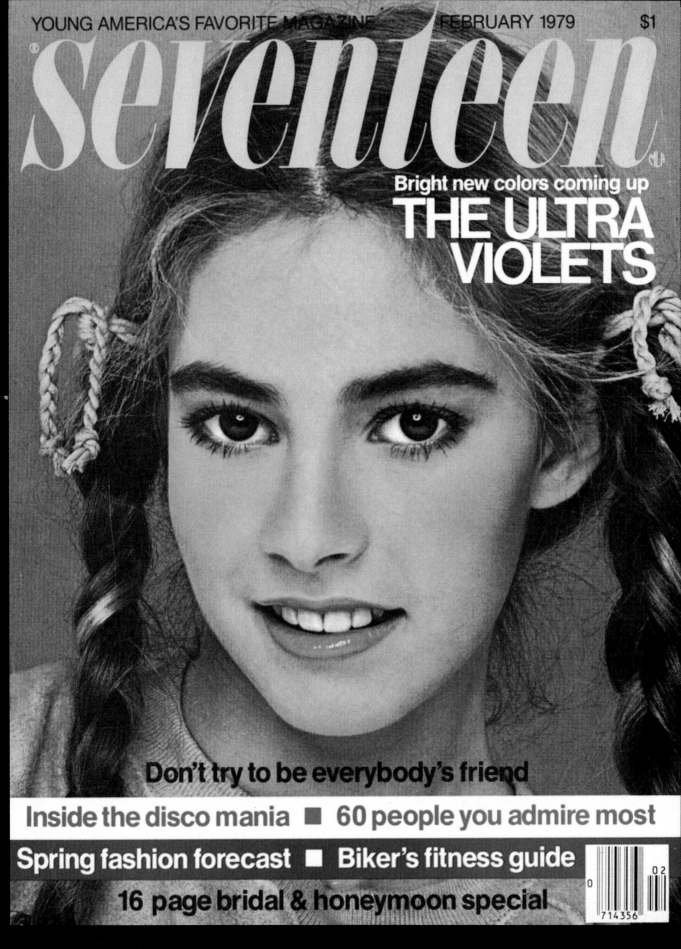

YOUNG AMERICA'S FAVORITE MAGAZINE   FEBRUARY 1979 $1

Seventeen

Bright new colors coming up
THE ULTRA VIOLETS

Don't try to be everybody's friend

Inside the disco mania ■ 60 people you admire most

Spring fashion forecast ■ Biker's fitness guide

16 page bridal & honeymoon special

714356

What if? Future thoughts

The day I knew it was going to be me on the February cover was the most exciting day of my life. At first, I was so shocked, I could hardly say anything. Then, after I left, I went straight to a phone and called my mom. She was as happy about it as I was. She told me not to get a big head about it, though. Being a cover girl is great, but you have to think about what's next. She made me realize there are always new goals to go for, no matter what you do. I'm sure there will be other good things that will happen if I keep on modeling, but right now that's a big if.

First of all, I might not even grow those extra two and a half inches I need to get into the Women's Division. And I can't do young teen stuff forever. So I think about that a lot. What if, someday, the bookings all stop because I'm too short? I think that would be a big disappointment. It's one thing if you decide not to model anymore. It's another thing if you can't—especially after you've done a lot of it. I keep thinking the photographers who like me now may not want to use me in the future. And I've got to face the fact that I could be a "has-been" pretty early in life. Covers or no.

But if there's one thing modeling teaches you, it's how to deal with rejection. You get it all the time—even when you're working regularly. There's always a client out there who doesn't like your look, and there's always a job you're going to lose to another model. Even, sometimes, after you've been booked for it. Those are the biggest disappointments. But clients cancel models, or shootings, all the time. That's just the way it works, so you soon learn not to get your hopes up for anything. A few times, I was all excited about location trips I had been tentatively booked to go on, and I had taken some tests at school early so I could go, and everything. At the last minute, they decided to take someone else. I have to admit, I felt pretty discouraged. But you just have to go on to the next job.

I can't help thinking what if, one day, there is no next job? I hope I'll be doing something else, and just glad that modeling taught me what it's like to be a career woman. I've had to learn how to be responsible for myself on my own, and how to deal with people in business, too. Because modeling is just a business. You work and you get paid for it. But by earning money early, you also have to learn how to manage it. The money can really spoil you. Because there aren't many jobs that pay so well, I guess my goals are going to be higher and harder for future careers. But I hope that modeling will be a good stepping-stone to whatever I may want to do.

Since Betsy's doing other things besides modeling now, I like to talk to her about different careers. Sometimes we do more talking than shoot-

ing. Like this day in the park. I asked her why she even started taking photographs. She said it started out as a hobby, but then it turned into a serious hobby. I know Betsy still likes to model, but mostly it's because of the people and the travel, and, naturally, the money. But she feels that she isn't using her whole self by just modeling. There are a lot of challenges to doing the job right, but once you master them, there are few new things to learn. And when you've really got it down, you hardly have to think about what you're doing.

I'm not at that point yet. But it makes me wonder. Even if I *do* grow, I might lose interest in modeling someday. Betsy says it's not a field you'd ever want to spend your whole life in. You can't go around worrying about how tall you are, or how much you weigh, or how pretty you are all the time. I don't, but I do wonder about what I'd like to do next. I always did want to be an archaeologist, ever since I saw a film about it in grade school. It looked exciting, and that's a field where you really do have to think about new things all the time.

Or maybe I could get into films. I know making commercials is fun, and I like the acting I've done in my theatre class. This summer, I'm even going to go to a good drama school in New York. They have a special program for kids and it's a pretty thorough course. We go two days a week and study speech, voice, movement, and acting technique. I really want to be ready for any acting jobs that come along. It's not always easy for models to get into films! For one thing, some models are only offered "pretty girl" roles and not taken seriously. And also, being a model doesn't automatically make you an actress. So I want to be sure I know what I'm doing.

Even without a lot of experience, I had a chance to do a movie last year. It was for one of the starring roles in a film directed by Randal Kleiser (he did *Grease*) with the cinematographer from *Days of Heaven*. It took place in the Fiji Islands at the turn of the century. These two kids, eight and nine years old, a boy and a girl, are on this sailing ship that sinks. They end up alone on an island and grow up there, and, you know, become aware of each other and make love. They're about to be rescued, but they've already eaten some poisonous berries, and—well—you'll be seeing it and I don't want to give away the ending. It's really a beautiful story, but I would have had to appear nude in some scenes. They would just have been distance shots, and they said they might use a stand-in, but I didn't want to take any chances. I talked it over with my mom, and we decided it would be better for me not to do it.

Whatever I do, though, I've found out what it takes to be a professional. You need enough discipline and patience to just keep at something until it's really right. And you have to take pride in what you're doing. I think modeling has helped me develop this attitude. And that's got to carry through to any other career I try.

I can see this kind of professional attitude in Betsy and her photographs. And the time she spends getting everything just right before she shoots. The camera angle, the lighting, the location—and, of course, me! Maybe one of these days she'll even teach me how to use a camera. Then I'll be able to say "Hey, Betsy, chin up a little more, lean a little more into the light, that's it, turn a little toward me. Okay, now, smile. . . . "

174